God's Creation
Help Tell the Story

illustrated by **Joanne Liu**

Can you help tell the story
of how God created the world?

Thank you!

What did God create first?
Clap your hands and see what happens!

First there was light.

Now slide your hand over
the page from left to right.

Good.
God called the dark night,

and he called the light day.
What would God create next?

Turn the page.

Interesting.
What is it?

Ready for more?

Shake the book from side to side.

Try tilting the book up.

A bit more.

Excellent.
Now we can see the sky at the top
and the sea at the bottom.

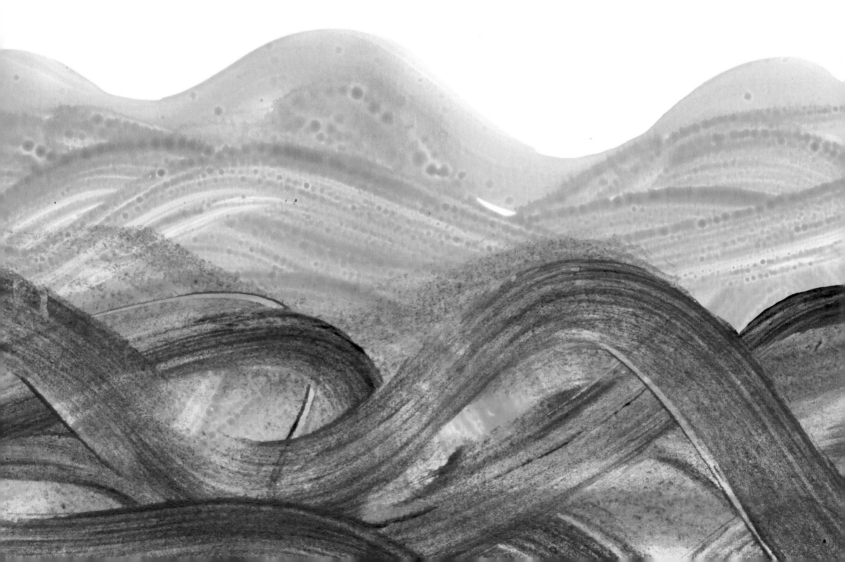

Better let the water settle down.

Amazing!
God called the brown part land.

Tap the brown.

Keep tapping!

Good!
Very Good!

Tap some more!

Beautiful.

Now that God had created the sky, the sea, and the land, he was ready to fill them with all sorts of amazing things.

Rub the sky to really heat it up.

It's the sun!
Let's see what else is hiding
up in the sky.

Push the sun down.
Be gentle, it only takes one finger ...

The moon, stars,
and planets!

Very good!
Aren't they beautiful?

Can you blow the stars across the sky?

Gorgeous.

Turn the page to see what God did next.

God filled the sea!

Can you pop the bubbles?

Wow!

The sea is now filled with lots
of cool sea creatures.

But wait, there's more.

Turn the page!

Finally!
Time to fill the land.

Give the book one good shake.

Whoa! Fun!

Shake it a few more times.

Very, very good.
But God still wasn't done.

Can you blow across the land very gently?

Again. But not too hard!

People!
Don't they look good?
God thought so too.

It was so good he decided to rest.

And that was just the beginning.